Roscoe The Volunteer EMT
Meets Titan the Police Officer

Story by
Jeremy Wenning

Art by
Jessica Vassar

Coco Publications

Published in 2016, by Coco Publications
Coldwater, OH 45828

Wenning, Jeremy
Roscoe the Volunteer EMT Meets Titan the Police Officer
Story by Jeremy Wenning Art by Jessica Vassar
ISBN
978-1-5323-1846-7
Library of Congress Control Number
2016916622

Edited by Lauren Wenning
Book Design by Jessica Vassar
PRINTED IN THE UNITED STATES OF AMERICA

This book is dedicated to all who serve the public; EMTs, Firefighters, & Police Officers. We all stand together when the going gets tough. This book is also dedicated to all of those who lost their lives in the line of duty.

Officer Titan was in the middle of his morning doughnut stop when a red convertible sports car went flying by!

Titan's doughnut fell out of his mouth and hit the ground as he headed to his cruiser. He chased down the red sports car and signaled the car to pull over.

Officer Titan was in the middle of the routine traffic stop, when he heard over the radio, "Injury accident at the intersection of Maple and Dogwood!" Titan gave Penny Turtle a warning for speeding. He hopped into his police car, turned on his lights and sirens, and headed to the scene.

Roscoe and Chief Clever were on ambulance call that day. They heard the siren and were heading to the accident with their lights and sirens blaring.

Roscoe and Clever were the first two to arrive.
Titan was right behind them.

He parked his police car to block any more traffic from coming down Maple Street. He took flares out of his trunk and lit them to warn drivers that they needed to slow down!

Roscoe and Clever headed over to the car. It was Rosemary Opossum. She had run off the road and hit a tree! Roscoe went to the driver's side door.

"Are you okay?" he asked her.

"Just my ankle," she replied.

Titan had the road blocked so he went over and asked Roscoe
if he could help. Clever motioned for Titan to go in the car
and hold Rosemary's head still. Titan went behind Rosemary
and put his paws under both of her ears to keep her head steady.

He put on the c-collar and then slowly and carefully loaded
Rosemary on the backboard. They secured her head
with the head chucks and strapped her on the backboard,
remembering to do the middle strap first.

Then they placed her on the cot, strapped her in, and loaded her into the ambulance. Roscoe took Rosemary's blood pressure, checked her pulses—all 4 of them–and wrapped her ankle to keep it still. Clever drove the ambulance to the hospital.

Titan arrived at the hospital just before Roscoe and Clever were getting ready to leave. The two EMTs went over to Titan.

"Thank you for your help," Clever said gratefully.

"No problem," Titan replied. "It is part of my duty to serve and protect the citizens of this community. We are all a team, and we need to work together to give quality service."

They shook hands, then Roscoe and Clever headed back to the squad house.

Titan went in to check on Rosemary to make sure she was fine. Rosemary thanked him.

Titan smiled and said, "It's all part of my job, Ma'am."

Titan left the hospital feeling appreciated.

God..

Grant me the ability
To give emergency care
With skillful hands, a knowledgeable mind
And tender love and care.
Help me deal with everthing,
When lives are on the line
To see the worst, administer aid,
And ease a worried mind.

So help me as I go today
Accept what fate may be
Touch these hands,
Use this mind,
Help this EMT

Amen.